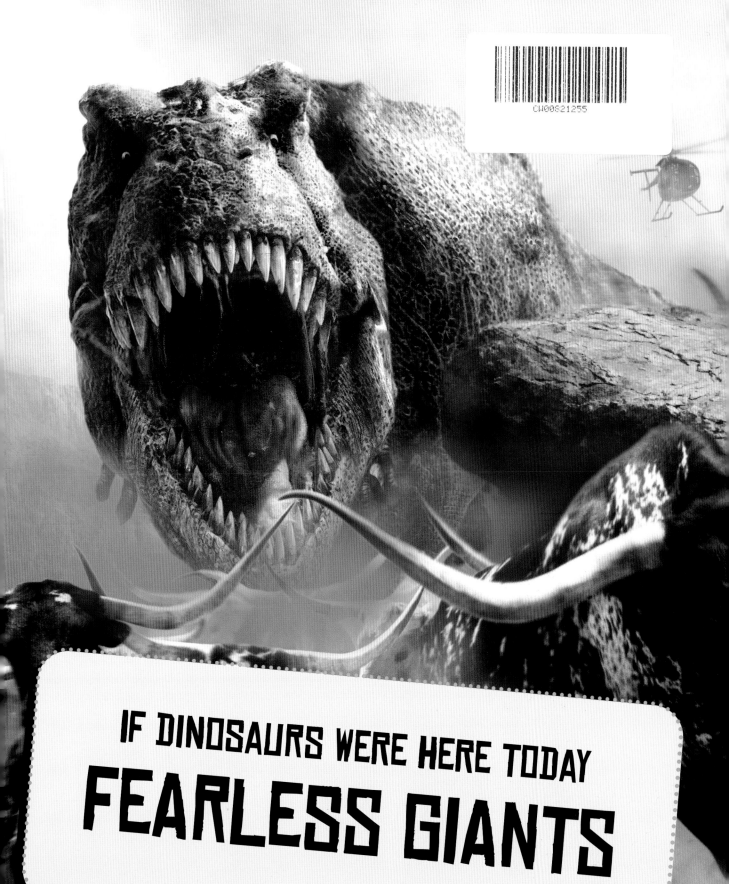

IF DINOSAURS WERE HERE TODAY

FEARLESS GIANTS

First published in 2024 by Hungry Tomato Ltd
F15, Old Bakery Studios, Blewetts Wharf, Malpas
Road, Truro, Cornwall,
TR1 1QH, UK.

A CIP catalogue record for this book is available from
the British Library.

ISBN 9781916598935

Printed in China

Discover more at
www.hungrytomato.com

Picture Credits:
(abbreviations: t=top, b=bottom, m=middle, l=left,
r=right, bg=background)

Alamy: Worldfoto 9bl, 14-15bg, 23tl. Ardea: Francois
Gohier 8br, 18-19bg. Getty Images: 12-13bg; Stone
3m, 9tr, 16-17bg, Taxi 1bg, 8bl. NaturePL: Neil
Lucas 2l, 9ml, 10-11bg. NHPA: Stephen Dalton 7mr.
Science Faction.net: Paul Bowen 4bg, 7bl, 9br, 20-
21bg. Shutterstock: 24tr; Alex Coan 26bl; AmeliAU
29tl; Catmando 8ml; ChameleonEye 30tr; Christian
Mvsat 23b; Daniel Eskridge 22b, 25b; David.costa.
art 6tl; Denis—S 6mr, 9mr; Elenarts 28bl; Giorgio
Rossi 28mr; Hans engbers 31tl; Herschel Hoffmeyer
7tl; Jaroslav Moravcik 30bl; JonathanC photography
7tl; Khadi Ganier 29bl; Kostiantyn Ivanyshen 8tr,
8mr; Maksim Shchur 31mr; Marcio Jose Bastos
Silva 27ml; Mark brandon 6bl; Michael Rosskothen
25mr; Microgen 29mr; Penny Hicks 31br; Puwadol
Jaturawutthichai 27tl; Tryoka 25tl; Warpaint 26tr;
WDnet Creation 3b, 22tl. Simon Mendez 8br, 9bl,
14-15bg, 18-19bg, 23tl.

Every effort has been made to trace the copyright
holders, and we apologise in advance for any
unintentional omissions. We would be pleased to
insert the appropriate acknowledgements in any
subsequent edition of this publication.

IF DINOSAURS WERE HERE TODAY!
FEARLESS GIANTS

by John Allan
Illustrated by Simon Mendez

HUNGRY TOMATO.

WARNING! These extinct beasts are not alive today. But just imagine if they were...

CONTENTS

Words in **BOLD** can be
found in the glossary.

THE STORY OF THE DINOSAURS

Planet Earth is around 4.5 billion years old. Rocks containing traces of living things shows us that there's been life on Earth for around 3.6 billion years. During Earth's long history, the planet and the creatures that roam it have changed drastically. We've all heard of the dinosaurs, but where did they come from, and where are they now?

WHEN DINOSAURS ROAMED

Dinosaurs were the most famous and fascinating animals to come from these prehistoric times. Dinosaurs were the biggest land-living creatures to have ever lived. Alongside these giants lived smaller, bird-like dinosaurs, flying reptiles and huge ocean-dwelling beasts.

Then, 65 million years ago, the dinosaurs were suddenly gone! Scientists believe that a huge asteroid hit Earth, wiping out most living things. The extinction of the dinosaurs allowed for the rise of new animals: 4 million years ago, humans appeared!

FOSSIL FINDS

Humans began observing rocks and, in the 1700s, discovered that the **fossils** they contained were the remains of ancient plants and animals. Fossil hunting became popular and the study of fossils – **palaeontology** – was born.

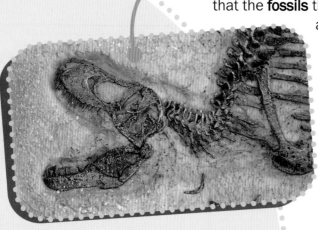

In 1842, scientist Sir Richard Owen invented the term 'Dinosauria' to describe the giant creatures that had once walked the Earth. Their remains fascinated both scientists and ordinary people – everyone wanted to know what these creatures had been like.

THEN AND NOW

For over two centuries, dinosaurs have amazed and fascinated us. We wonder how they'd compare to the animals of today.

How vast would a towering Sauroposeidon seem alongside today's biggest land-living animal, the African elephant?

Could these ancient **herbivores** survive eating today's plants and competing with today's animals?

And would prehistoric ocean predators be big enough to attack and kill modern-day whales?

THE UNKNOWN

We may never know exactly what it would be like to live with dinosaurs. We can only imagine, taking what we've discovered from their fossilised remains, and comparing it to what we know about modern animals to picture what life would be like if dinosaurs were here today!

If you've got the courage, read on...
...be prepared for some truly bizarre and spine-tingling - though imaginary - encounters between human or animal and beast.

TIMELINE

CRETACEOUS PERIOD
[145–66 MILLION YEARS AGO]

This was when some of the most famous dinosaurs lived, including T.rex, Triceratops and Spinosaurus. Who knows what other dinosaurs would have lived since then if they hadn't all been wiped out by the huge meteorite?

TRIASSIC PERIOD
[252–201 MILLION YEARS AGO]

Dinosaurs appeared towards the end of the Triassic **period**. They tended to live by the seaside, along riverbanks and in desert **oases** where water was plentiful. Early dinosaurs included Plateosaurus and Shonisaurus.

JURASSIC PERIOD
[201–145 MILLION YEARS AGO]

During the Jurassic period, Earth's climate became moister and milder – new plants and forests grew, meaning new food sources for plant-eating dinos. As a result, both plant- and meat-eating dinosaurs started to grow much bigger.

SHONISAURUS

Name meaning 'lizard from the Shoshone mountains' – after the North American mountains where its fossils were first found.

Fossils of many sea creatures have been found high in mountains around the world which shows that some mountains were once under the sea!

LIOPLEURODON

Name meaning 'smooth-sided tooth'.

This prehistoric **carnivore** may have had a stronger bite than Tyrannosaurus! Although it coexisted with the dinos, it's unrelated to them and is instead classed as a **pliosaur** - a type of marine reptile.

TYRANNOSAURUS REX

Name meaning 'tyrant lizard'.

Often referred to as T.rex, this is one of the most famous dinos. The earliest Tyrannosaurus' (during the Jurassic period) were turkey-sized animals, but by the Late Cretaceous period, they'd become some of the biggest meat-eaters ever known.

MOSASAURUS

Name meaning 'lizard from the Meuse' – after the Netherlands rivers where the first specimen was found.

This giant was one of the most powerful hunters to live at the end of the Age of Dinosaurs.

MASS EXTINCTION

For millions of years, dinosaurs ruled the Earth, until there was a **mass extinction**. There is evidence that a **meteorite** struck Earth around 65 million years ago, exploding rock fragments, causing **tsunamis** and forest fires, resulting in the death of the dinosaurs and all other reptiles of the time.

SAUROPOSEIDON

Name meaning 'lizard of Poseidon' – after the ancient Greek earthquake god.

This huge creature belonged to the **sauropod** (lizard-footed) dinosaurs – a group of plant-eaters with long necks. They are the biggest land-living animals ever discovered.

QUETZALCOATLUS

Name comes from 'Quetzalcoatl' which was a flying serpent-god in Aztec mythology.

Despite living in the Age of Dinosaurs, and sharing some similarities, this large creature isn't a dinosaur, but rather a **pterosaur** - a flying reptile.

CAUGHT UP
MOSASAURUS

A drift net closes around a shoal of ammonites. The swimming molluscs bunch together as the walls of their trap close around them. Then the net is gathered, and the whole catch is lifted from the water. But ammonites are not the only things caught. A Mosasaurus – a massive swimming lizard that had been hunting the ammonites – is tangled in the net as well. An unsuspecting victim of the fishing industry.

The **mosasaurs** were closely related to today's monitor lizards, but were completely aquatic. We know that they ate ammonites because we've found fossil ammonite shells that had been bitten many times and crushed by mosasaurus jaws, while the reptile extracted the soft-bodied animal from within. They would be as at home in modern oceans as they were at the end of the Age of Dinosaurs.

MOSASAURUS
PRONOUNCED
mo-suh-saw-rus

LIVED
Late Cretaceous period
70-65 million years ago

LENGTH
up to 17 metres (57ft)

DIET
Piscivore

FAMOUS FINDS

Before dinosaurs were discovered, people found the remains of some huge, extinct sea animals. The picture below shows one of the most famous Mosasaurus' which was dug up in a Dutch quarry in 1780. The fossil was seized in a subsequent war and taken to Paris as loot. It was studied there by the most famous **naturalist** of the day, Baron Georges Cuvier.

FAMILY TIES

The prehistoric Mosasaurus may be a relative of the **Ice Age** Megalania, and the Komodo dragon that's found in Indonesia today. Whereas the Mosasaurus was a sea-dwelling animal, the others are land animals.

GIANT OF THE DEEP
SHONISAURUS

From the dark depths of the ocean, a mighty Shonisaurus rises towards the pale blue glow of the upper waters. Its watchful eye spots a giant octopus, lazily flapping along, with a bunching and opening of its tentacles. The great jaws close, and the giant octopus is gone.

Although often mistaken for dinosaurs, prehistoric marine reptiles like Shonisaurus were actually separate types of creatures. Shonisaurus was an **ichthyosaur** - a fish-shaped reptile of the Age of Dinosaurs. The earliest ones seem to have been the largest. In the Triassic period they were as enormous as some modern-day sperm whales. They probably lived like sperm whales as well, eating the biggest of the marine **invertebrates** of the time. A huge one, like Shonisaurus, would find plenty to eat in today's oceans.

SHONISAURUS
PRONOUNCED
show-nee-saw-rus

LIVED
Late Triassic Period around 220-205 million years ago

LENGTH
21 metres (69ft)

DIET
Piscivore

MODERN GIANTS
People think that prehistoric animals were bigger than anything alive today. However, that's not true. The modern-day blue whale still holds the title of the biggest ocean creature to have ever existed.

SEA MONSTER
A huge Shonisaurus jaw bone was discovered in 2018 which was around 20% larger than previously found fossils, which suggests that Shonisaurus may have been even bigger than we thought! There were probably other monster ichthyosaurs that we haven't discovered yet. Obviously something about the oceans in Triassic times encouraged the growth of these very big creatures. The ichthyosaurs existed for another 120 million years after this period. But the later ichthyosaurs were more modest dolphin-sized animals.

GIANT OF THE PLAINS
SAUROPOSEIDON

The hot sun beats down on the burning, dry plains. A herd of elephants gather at a watering hole to drink and bathe. Each of the giant mammals weighs more than 50 men and stands at over 3 metres (10ft) tall. They push and splash, enjoying the cooling water. Suddenly, a monstrous creature that dwarfs even the largest elephant in the herd towers over them. A huge Sauroposeidon is wading into the shallow water. Twice as tall at the shoulder and ten times heavier than the biggest of the elephants, the great dinosaur moves among the tusked giants.

Thanks to its incredibly long neck, Sauroposeidon is thought to be the tallest animal to have ever walked on Earth. It certainly dwarfed most of the other animals on the open plains of the Early Cretaceous world. It fed on tall trees, like the giraffe, and was a member of the sauropod group of long-necked plant-eaters. The elephants move away, but are in no danger from this vast, gentle herbivore – unless it accidently knocks one of them over with its massive tail!

SAUROPOSEIDON
PRONOUNCED
sore-oh-pos-eye-dun

LIVED
Early Cretaceous Period around 118-110 million years ago

LENGTH
up to 34 metres (110ft)

DIET
Herbivore

DINO DETECTIVE

Palaeontologists used the dimensions and shapes of Brachiosaurus neck bones to work out that Sauroposeidon was an animal that looked very much like Brachiosaurus, but was much bigger.

LONG NECKS

When the first Sauroposeidon fossils were found, palaeontologists thought that they were fossils of tree trunks because they were so big! The scientists eventually realised that the fossils were neck **vertebrae**. Based on the size of the vertebrae - amongst the biggest ever uncovered - Sauroposeidon's neck is estimated to be around 12 metres (39ft) long!

A TERRIBLE TYRANT
TYRANNOSAURUS REX

Wild cattle are grazing peacefully on the open plains. Suddenly, one animal senses danger and snorts a warning. The herd scatters. A mighty Tyrannosaurus has been lying in wait for them. It's now bearing down on them, its powerful jaws, armed with huge teeth, opening for the kill. A film crew captures the scene from a helicopter above.

Many palaeontologists believe that this is how the fearsome predator Tyrannosaurus hunted its prey. Others think Tyrannosaurus was too big and heavy to sneak up on and chase its prey, and would've feasted on the corpses of animals that had already died instead. The most likely story is that both of these theories are true – Tyrannosaurus was an active hunter, but wouldn't have missed the chance to scavenge on **carrion**, or steal a meal from a rival predator. Whatever its choice of food, Tyrannosaurus would probably find itself hunted to extinction by farmers trying to protect their livestock even if it had survived the meteorite 65 million years ago.

TYRANNOSAURUS REX
PRONOUNCED
tie-ran-uh-saw-rus rex

LIVED
Late Cretaceous period 68–65 million years ago

LENGTH
up to 13 metres (42ft)

DIET
Carnivore

POWERFUL JAWS
Tyrannosaurus skulls were massive, with mouths that could hold whole cows! Tyrannosaurus' powerful jaws and teeth could penetrate the thick skin of a dinosaur, such as Triceratops, and crunch through its bones in a single bite.

TYRANT TEETH
A Tyrannosaurus tooth could grow up to 30cm (1ft), including the root – that's three times the length of a lion's tooth!

MARINE MONSTER
LIOPLEURODON

As seals bask close to the shore, an orca suddenly beaches to attack the unsuspecting animals. Unsuccessful, the orca prepares to slide back into the water with the pull of the next wave but, slowly and silently, an even bigger predator approaches. Suddenly the water seems to boil as the vast jaws of Liopleurodon break the surface and the most monstrous hunter the world has ever known moves in for the kill.

Liopleurodon cruised the Jurassic seas propelled by four large flippers. This giant pliosaur was a powerful swimmer and its massive jaws and huge teeth made it a fearsome hunter. Liopleurodon had only one enemy – its own kind! Like today's sperm whales, orcas, and great white sharks, it was the top predator in its **habitat**, killing and eating any other living thing that came within its reach. It would probably be one of the top predators in today's oceans.

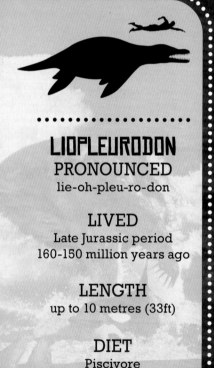

LIOPLEURODON

PRONOUNCED
lie-oh-pleu-ro-don

LIVED
Late Jurassic period
160-150 million years ago

LENGTH
up to 10 metres (33ft)

DIET
Piscivore

OVERSIZED GIANT

Previous estimations of Liopleurodon's length suggested it grew to 25 metres (82ft) long. Palaeontologists generally consider this to be an exaggeration. As of yet, no fossil evidence supports the creature being that large. But perhaps it could have grown that large if it fed on our modern-day ocean dwellers...

KEEN NOSE

Palaeontologists believe that Liopleurodon could smell its prey in the water. They think it used its forward-facing nostrils to locate other creatures and pinpoint them, even if they were out of sight. Like the modern-day great white shark, Liopleurodon could probably smell a potential meal from a great distance.

THE SUPER VULTURE
QUETZALCOATLUS

For some time, the pilot of a small passenger plane has been trying to fly away from a huge pair of Quetzalcoatlus. He may have flown too close to their nest, or they may just be enjoying the thrill of a chase. As the pilot banks to avoid making contact with them, he notices another plane ahead. The situation is getting quite dangerous...

Amongst the **pterosaurs**, Quetzalcoatlus was one of the biggest, with a wingspan exceeding that of many hang gliders and even some powered aircraft. Most pterosaur fossils have been found by the sea, leading us to believe that this was their primary habitat. Quetzalcoatlus, however, lived well inland, where it was able to use rising air **thermals** from the warm, open landscape to keep it aloft for vast distances. Quetzalcoatlus would dominate the skies today, and probably compete with vultures for dead animals on the ground.

QUETZALCOATLUS
PRONOUNCED
ket-sul-ko-at-lus

LIVED
Late Cretaceous period
70-65 million years ago.

WINGSPAN
up to 11 metres (36ft)

DIET
Carnivore

GLIDER
The exact wingspan of Quetzalcoatlus is unknown. Only part of a wing skeleton has been found, which suggests a wingspan of between 10-12 metres (33-40ft). Despite being such a huge animal, the Quetzalcoatlus is thought to have been quite light, weighing less than 250kg (550lbs).

GIANT WINGSPAN
The albatross has the biggest wingspan of any modern bird – 3.5 metres (12ft). However, even it would be dwarfed by the size of these gigantic pterosaurs.

DINOSAUR AWARDS

Dinosaurs were the biggest land-living creatures that ever walked the Earth, but whilst some would tower over trees and buildings if they lived today, it might surprise you to find out that they weren't all huge! Let's find out which ones deserve recognition for their impressive size.

Compsognathus

SMALLEST CARNIVORE

One of the most famous small dinosaurs is the Compsognathus which grew to be around the size of a chicken! For many years, it was considered to be the smallest carnivorous dino, however, recent fossil discoveries of even smaller dinos suggest this title needs updating!

LONGEST TAIL

The longest tails belonged to dinos in the **diplodocidae** family which included Diplodocus, Seismosaurus, and Supersaurus. Fossils discovered in 2021 suggest that Supersaurus had the longest tail, measuring 18 metres (60ft).

Diplodocae dinosaur

TALLEST DINO

Palaeontologists think that Sauroposeidon was the tallest dinosaur. Only four neck bones have ever been found but by analysing those and the proportions of the closely related Brachiosaurus, they've estimated that it was over 18 metres (60ft)!

Sauroposeidon

LONGEST NECK

Did you think giraffes had long necks? Then you should have seen some of the dinosaurs that used to walk the Earth! The longest dino neck overall belonged to Mamenchisaurus which is estimated to have been 15 metres (49ft) long.

Mamenchisaurus

THE LIVES OF DINOSAURS TODAY

Both humans and dinosaurs would lead completely different lives if we existed alongside each other. Imagine walking through the park and seeing a ginormous plant-eater munching on the tops of the trees or seeing a huge pterosaur, bigger than a plane, zoom overhead! What do you think would be the biggest change to your day-to-day life?

PROTECT THE PLESIOSAURS!

How exactly would huge **plesiosaurs**, like Mosasaurus, affect marine life today? Would they be a nuisance, eating so many fish to fuel their massive bodies that we would see mass extinction of smaller fish species? Or would we treasure their presence in our seas and have to protect them from humans hunting them for trophies, as we protect endangered sharks and whales?

POOR AIR

Pterosaurs, like Quetzalcoatlus, may not have been able to survive in today's **atmosphere**. Some scientists think that the mixture of gases in the air was different during the **Mesozoic Era**. It's possible that the level of oxygen or carbon dioxide was higher than it is today. This may affect pterosaurs' ability to fly.

NESTS AND EGGS

Birds today take time to build nests in trees, lay hard-shelled eggs, and nurture their young that need help preparing for adulthood. Pterosaurs, on the other hand, didn't make complex nests but are thought to have buried their soft-shelled eggs in the ground to protect them. It's thought that they buried them in huge nesting sites with other pterosaur eggs, similar to modern sea turtle nests. Their eggs would be at risk from modern predators like wolves.

SHARK OR DINOSAUR

If you saw an ichthyosaur, like Shonisaurus, in the distance, you would think it was a dolphin, or a shark. It had the same streamlined shape, half-moon fin on its tail and possibly even a triangular fin on its back. Whilst the largest of these animals could survive in today's world, the smaller of the species may be at risk from over-fishing or over-hunting, as our modern sea animals are.

DID YOU KNOW?

Dinosaurs are fascinating creatures. Scientists are constantly discovering more about them and finding answers to the world's most curious questions. Did you know these amazing facts about dinosaurs?

HOW LONG WAS THE LIFESPAN OF THE AVERAGE DINOSAUR?

It varied. Small meat-eaters were probably quite short-lived. Large meat-eaters like Tyrannosaurus lived to be about 30. The big sauropods may have lived to be over 100. However, life was hard in dinosaur times, and it would have been rare for a dinosaur to live long.

HOW BIG WAS DINO DUNG?

Fossilised dino dung called 'coprolite' tells us what the dinosaurs ate. It's usually harder to find complete plant-eater poops as they tended to get broken up and scattered. They were probably like monster-size cow plops. Meat-eater poops are like those of cats and dogs – more compact. Palaeontologists have found a huge 67cm (2.2ft) long Tyrannosaurus coprolite full of dinosaur bones.

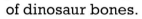

HOW MANY BONES DID A TYRANNOSAURUS HAVE?

We don't know as we have never found a complete skeleton.

WHICH DINOSAUR HAD THE BIGGEST TEETH?

The longest recorded tooth belonged to T.rex. It measured a terrifying 30cm (12in) from root to tip!

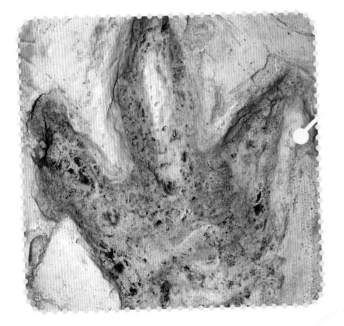

WHAT SIZE IS THE BIGGEST DINOSAUR FOOTPRINT?

A big sauropod footprint found recently in Australia is almost 1.75 metres (5ft 9in) long. But it's impossible to say exactly what dinosaur made them.

HOW WOULD A LONG NECK HELP A DINOSAUR?

Like the hose of a vacuum cleaner, it would reach around for food without having to move its heavy body.

TRUE OR FALSE?

There are a lot of fun facts about dinosaurs but what is actually true and what is a myth? Put your dino knowledge to the test with this true or false quiz.

TYRANNOSAURUS WAS THE MOST POWERFUL DINOSAUR EVER!

FALSE. Whilst T.rex had the strongest bite, the most powerful was likely one of the biggest sauropods, like Argentinosaurus or Sauroposeidon. They had to be very powerful to move their great weights around.

ALL DINOSAURS LIVED AT THE SAME TIME!

FALSE. The Age of Dinosaurs lasted for millions of years. During this time, hundreds of different species lived and then became extinct, allowing for more dinos to grow and roam. It's estimated that Stegosaurus had been extinct for around 80 million years before Tyrannosaurus appeared.

SOME DINOSAURS TOOK LONGER THAN OTHERS TO GROW FROM BABY TO ADULT!

TRUE. Some plant-eaters grew much quicker than their predators. For example, Hypacrosaurus reached its full adult size in 10 years. Whereas T.rex grew steadily until it was about 14 years old. Then it grew quickly until it reached its adult size at 18, and died by 30.

DINOSAURS LIVED IN DIFFERENT PLACES AROUND THE WORLD!

TRUE. Each creature lived in different areas. They adapted to their landscapes, climates, and food sources which kept them in one type of habitat. Because of this, many dinosaurs would never have met each other.

DINOSAUR FOSSILS HAVE BEEN FOUND ON ALL CONTINENTS OF THE WORLD!

TRUE. Palaeontologists have discovered fossils across the world, on every **continent** and in many different countries.

THE LOCH NESS MONSTER IS A DINOSAUR!

FALSE. No dinosaurs lived in water. Creatures that lived in water during the Age of Dinosaurs were plesiosaurs or pliosaurs - reptiles that were well-adapted to water-living with streamlined bodies and heads, and paddle-shaped limbs. If the Loch Ness Monster exists, it may have features that would allow it to live in water, but that wouldn't necessarily make it a plesiosaur or pliosaur either.

UNCOVERING THE PAST

Can we see live dinosaurs today? Yes, if we count birds as dinosaurs. No, if we're thinking about the big dinosaurs in this book. In this case, we must rely on fossil evidence to tell us what they looked like. Since the 1820s, when the first dinosaur fossils were found, we've been building up our knowledge piece by piece (literally).

Our knowledge of dinosaurs is far from complete: it's very rare for scientists to uncover fossils. Not only are fossils usually deep underground, but it's rare for land-living animals to fossilise in the first place. To fossilise, the animal needs to have been buried quickly, otherwise bones get scattered and rot away from exposure to weather and **bacteria**.

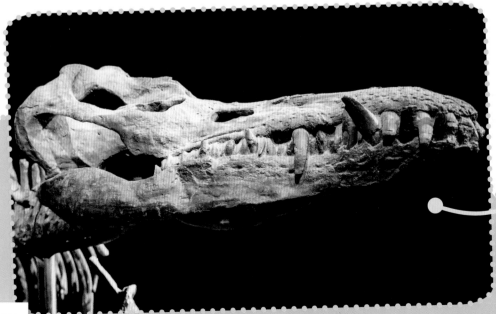

The first Liopleurodon fossils to be found were several of its huge teeth back in the 1800s. The dino was named after its teeth before scientists knew more about what it looked like!

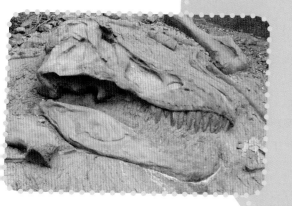

Fossils can be discovered in different circumstances. Usually, we only find isolated fossil bones which have been separated from the rest of the skeleton. They're not entirely useless - even an isolated tooth or limb bone may be identifiable to a species. However, because the bone has spent millions of years in the ground, it's often weathered or fragmented, making it tricky to find out which dinosaur it came from.

Scientists are discovering new prehistoric species all the time. Quetzalcoatlus is still a relatively new species, having been first discovered in the 1970s.

Only very occasionally are articulated skeletons uncovered – this is when the bones are still joined together, as they were in life. More commonly, associated skeletons are found – this is when the bones are jumbled up, but it's obvious that they came from the same animal. It takes a very knowledgeable scientist to put the bones back together.

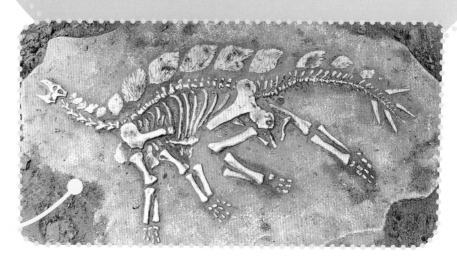

Articulated skeleton of a Stegosaurus.

ANYONE CAN FIND A FOSSIL!

You don't need to be a professional palaeontologist to discover a prehistoric creature. Many have been found by children. In 2021, a young girl discovered a 220-million-year-old dinosaur footprint! Given that dinosaurs appeared 230 million years ago, this footprint must be from one of the earliest dinosaurs to walk the Earth.

Perhaps the greatest fossil hunter of all was 12-year-old Mary Anning, who found and **excavated** the first complete skeleton of the prehistoric marine reptile Ichthyosaurus in England in 1811.

Why not begin your own searches by joining a fossil-hunting group?

Statue of Mary Anning, fossil hunter in Lyme Regis, Dorset (England).

INDEX

GLOSSARY

Atmosphere - The layer of gases which surround the Earth.

Bacteria - Microscopic organisms that can cause disease.

Carnivore - An animal that eats only meat.

Carrion - The decaying flesh of a dead animal.

Continent - One of the world's large expanses of land.

Diplodocidae – A group of plant-eating dinosaurs that had very long bodies, necks and tails.

Excavate (verb) - The careful removal of earth from an area in order to find buried remains.

Fossil - The remains or impression of a prehistoric plant or animal embedded in rock and preserved.

Habitat – The place or environment where a plant or animal naturally lives or grows.

Herbivore - An animal which eats only plants.

Ice Age - A period of time when climates were much cooler than they are now and thick sheets of ice called glaciers covered most of Earth's land.

Ichthyosaur - A type of swimming reptile from the Mesozoic Era. They had streamlined fish-like bodies with fins and a tail.

Invertebrate - An animal without a backbone.

Mass extinction - An event that brings about the extinction of a large number of animals and plants. There have been about five mass extinctions in the history of life on Earth.

Meteorite - A rock from space.

Mesozoic Era – The era of time in which dinosaurs lived, among other animals. It lasted around 186 million years, from 252 to 66 million years ago.

Mosasaur - A type of swimming reptile of the Cretaceous period, closely related to modern monitor lizards.

Naturalist – Someone who studies natural history (plants and animals).

Oases - Green areas in a desert, where there is water and plants grow.

Palaeontology - The study of ancient life and fossils. People who study this are called palaeontologists.

Period - A division of geological time that can be defined by the types of animals or plants that existed then. Typically, a period lasts for tens of millions of years.

Piscivore - An animal which eats mostly fish.

Plesiosaur - A large marine reptile of the Mesozoic Era, with large, paddle-like limbs and a long, flexible neck.

Pliosaur - A type of plesiosaur with a short neck, large head and massive, toothed jaws.

Pterosaur - One of a group of flying reptiles from the Mesozoic Era. They flew with leathery wings supported by an elongated finger. Pterodactylus was a pterosaur.

Sauropod – A type of extremely large herbivorous dinosaur that had a long neck and tail, trunk-like legs, but small head.

Thermals - Warm rising currents of air.

Tsunami – An extremely long and high fast-moving sea wave caused by an earthquake or other disturbance.

Vertebrae – The bones that make up an animal's spine.

PLANTS:
WHY DO WE NEED THEM?

Annabel Griffin

Illustrated by Tjarda Borsboom

Picture Credits:
Abbreviations: m-middle, t-top, l-left, r-right, bg-background.

Shutterstock: Bachkova Natalia 18tr; Dennis van de water 20tr; Forestman71 23br; GUDKOV
ANDREY 19tr; Kiran Nagarae 23tr; Knelson20 23mr; Leighton collins 23tl; Leungchopan 23ml;
Pangram 23bl; Skyrpnykov Dmytro 21ml; Tao Jiang 18bl; Visharo 20bl; Yakov Oskanov 19bl.

Copyright © 2024 Hungry Tomato Ltd

First published in 2024 by Hungry Tomato Ltd
F15, Old Bakery Studios, Blewetts Wharf, Malpas Road, Truro,
Cornwall,
TR1 1QH, UK.

A CIP catalogue record for this book is available from the British
Library.

ISBN 9781916598904

Printed in China

Discover more at
www.hungrytomato.com

Contents

Words in **BOLD** can be found in the glossary.

What Is a Plant?

Plants are living things that can be found almost everywhere on Earth! There are over 300,000 different types of plants on our planet. How many can you name?

Plants come in all sorts of shapes and sizes, but most of them have the same three parts: stem, roots, and leaves.

Stem

A plant's stem grows above the ground and gives support. It acts as a drinking straw for the plant, carrying water and **nutrients** from the roots to different parts of the plant.

Leaves

Leaves are very important. They help the plant make its own food, to give it energy and help it grow.

Roots

Roots are usually hidden underground. They help to hold the plant in place, like an anchor. They also take up water and nutrients from the soil that the plant needs to grow.

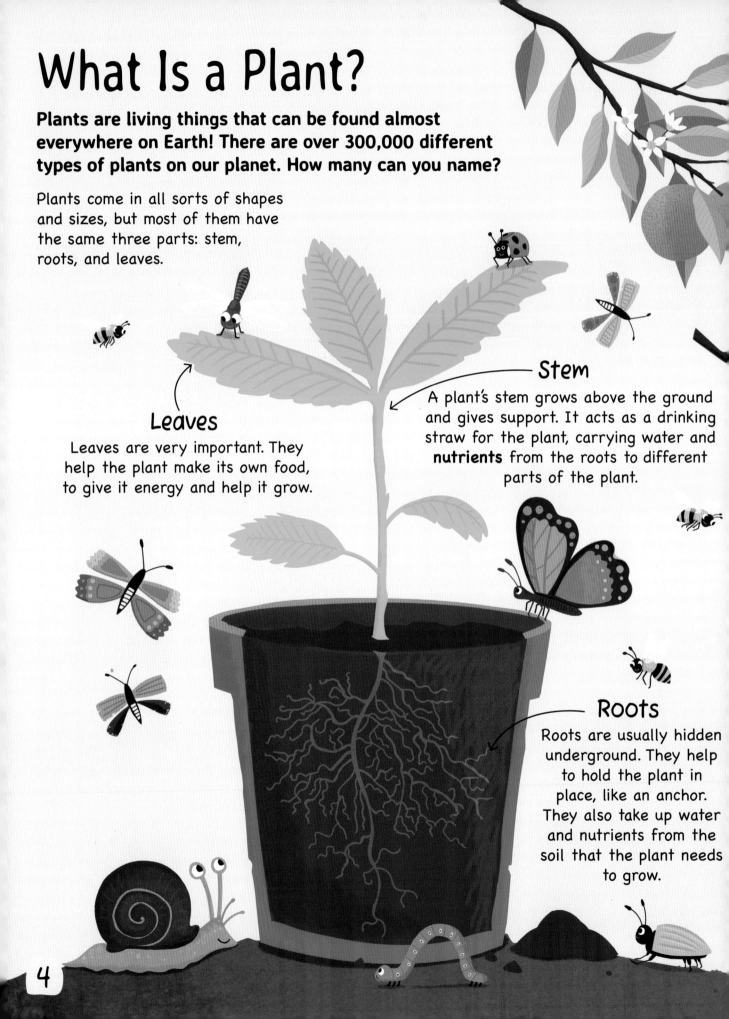

Blossom

Fruit

Berries

Some plants have other features, such as fruit, flowers, thorns, and branches.

Nuts

Flower

Petals

Thorns

Branches

Trunk

Now we know what a plant is, let's find out why they're so important!

5

Plants at Home

You probably have lots of things made from plants all over your home.

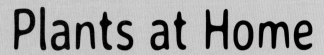

Toiletries

Soap, shampoo, perfume and make-up often contain parts of plants.

Outside

People with gardens often grow plants for decoration, for food, or to help wildlife.

Heating

Wood is sometimes burned for heat.

Building
Wood from trees is often used to build parts of houses.

House plants
Having plants inside can make your home look great!

Clothing
Clothing and some fabrics, like cotton, can be made from plants.

Books
Paper is made from wood. Without plants, books wouldn't exist!

Food
Fruits, vegetables and cereals come from plants.

Furniture
Chairs, tables, beds, storage and other furniture is often made from wood.

Useful Plants

Some plants are really handy for turning into useful or beautiful things. Did you know that all of these things are made from plants?

Bamboo

Bamboo is used to make all sorts of things, from houses to toothbrushes. It is fast and easy to grow. Pandas also love it!

Rubber

When a rubber tree's **bark** is cut, it oozes a milky **sap**, called latex. People collect the latex and use it to make rubber. Rubber is used to make all kinds of things, such as balloons.

Perfume

Flowers that smell nice are often used to make perfumes, soaps and other toiletries.

HAND SOAP

Fabrics

Some plants produce threads that can be spun into yarn, and used to make fabric.

Cotton

Cotton plants grow soft, white, fluffy balls of thread, which can be used to make cotton fabric.

Linen

Linen is another popular fabric. It's made from flax plants.

Dyes

Some plants can be used to dye fabrics different colours.

Indigo

The leaves of the indigo plant are used to dye fabrics blue. Denim was traditionally dyed with indigo.

Henna

Leaves from this plant are dried and crushed into a powder to make henna. Henna can be used to dye fabrics, hair, and even skin for special occasions, such as weddings.

9

Good and Bad

People have been using plants to create medicines for centuries. Some plants have the power to both heal and harm, depending on how they are used.

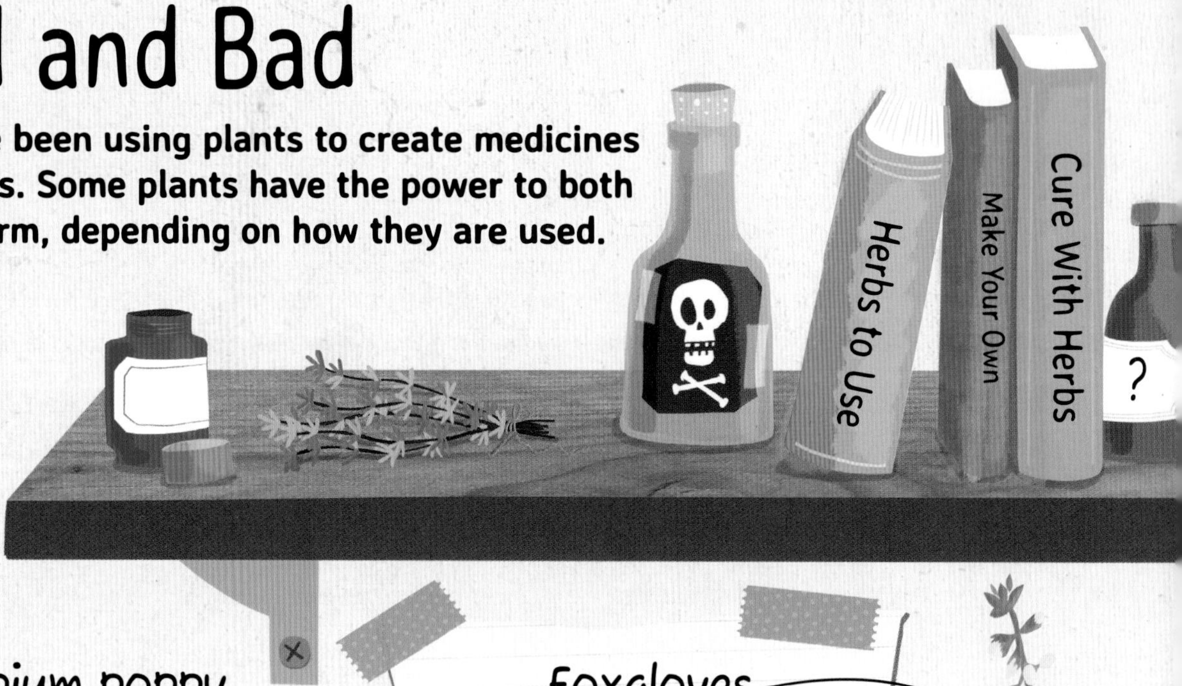

Herbs to Use

Make Your Own

Cure With Herbs

?

Opium poppy

A milky liquid found in some poppies is used to make pain-relief medicine.

Foxgloves

Foxgloves are very poisonous plants, and can make people very sick! However, they also have something in them that can be used as medicine to help treat people with heart failure.

Yew

Yews are **evergreen** trees with red berries. Yew is poisonous, but its bark has been used in medicines to help treat cancer.

Rose periwinkle

This plant grows in Madagascar. It has been used to make medicine to help fight cancer.

Willow bark

The bark of a willow tree is a natural medicine. It's kind to our bodies and is often used to cure a nasty headache!

Aloe vera

Gel from inside the aloe vera plant can be used to help soothe burns, rashes and dry skin.

St. John's Wort

St. John's wort has a history of use in herbal medicine dating back to ancient Greece.

Feeling Hungry?

Many different plants can be grown for food.
Fruits and vegetables are an important part of
a healthy diet.

Fruits
Fruits and berries usually
grow on trees or bushes. They
are often sweet and juicy.

Tomato

That Leaf
Looks tasty!

Leaves
The leaves of some
plants, like lettuce,
cabbages and spinach,
are great to munch on.

Seeds and pods
Some tasty vegetables, like peas and sweetcorn, are really the seeds of their plant.

Fruit or veg?
Some foods that we call vegetables are actually the fruits of a plant, including pumpkins, cucumbers and tomatoes.

Roots
Vegetables, such as carrots and beetroot, grow underground. They are the large, tasty roots of the plant.

Bulbs
Onions and garlic are actually **bulbs.**

Herbs and Spices

Some plants are used to add extra seasoning or spice. Spices usually come from the seeds, fruit, roots or bark of a plant, whereas herbs are from the leaves or stems.

Saffron

Saffron is the most expensive spice in the world. It comes from the flower of the saffron crocus.

Black pepper

Pepper is used to season lots of dishes. Peppercorns are tiny fruit that are usually dried and then crushed or ground into food.

Chilli pepper

Both the fruit and its seeds can be used to add "heat" and spice to food.

Cinnamon

Cinnamon is a spice that comes from the bark of a cinnamon tree. It is often used in hot drinks and baking.

Ginger

Ginger is a knobbly root that is used in both sweet and savoury dishes. It can be used fresh or dried.

Chives

Chives are related to onions and garlic. Their leaves have a similar taste, but aren't as strong.

Chives

Mint

Lots of things taste like mint. It can also be used as medicine, to settle stomach ache!

Rosemary

Rosemary leaves can be used as a fresh or dried herb.

Rosemary

Basil

Basil leaves are used in lots of dishes around the world.

PESTO
Alla genovese

Grow Your Own Chive Head

Chives can be used in salads and cooking.

You will need:

- Flowerpot
- Soil/peat-free potting compost
- Chive seeds
- Paints/pens
- Plastic eyes
- Glue
- Scissors

1. Decorate your pot using pens or paints, and plastic eyes.

Chive Seeds

2. Fill your pot with compost and plant your seeds, following the instructions on the seed packet.

3. Put your pot on a tray and place it on a sunny windowsill. Keep it well watered.

4. Once it is over 15cm tall, give your plant a haircut and use the cut chives in your cooking!

Planet Savers

Plants play a really important part in keeping our planet healthy.

Clean air

Plants take in **carbon dioxide** from the air and release **oxygen** through their leaves, which humans and other animals need to breathe.

$$CO_2$$

Too much carbon dioxide can lead to **global warming**! Planting more trees and plants will help to stop that happening.

Beautiful world

Plants help to make the world a beautiful place to be! Spending time in nature makes people happy.

Animal habitats

Trees and other plants are perfect **habitats** for animals. They provide food, shelter, and homes.

O^2

Clean water

Plants help to keep water clean by absorbing nutrients that could **pollute** it. Big plants, like trees, help to control the amount of rain that falls, reducing **droughts** and **flooding.**

Healthy soil

Fallen leaves and dead plants add nutrients back into the soil, keeping it healthy so that other plants can grow.

Why Do Animals Need Plants?

Lots of animals rely on plants for their food, homes and shelter.
How many can you think of?

Frog homes

Many frogs lay their eggs (called frogspawn) in ponds sheltered by reeds and other plants. This is a safe place for their babies to grow.

High and safe

Birds build their nests in trees to stay safely out of the reach of prowling predators, such as foxes and wolves.

Desert shelters

There's not much shelter in the desert, so Gila woodpeckers and little elf owls make their nests inside cacti.

Clever camouflage

Clever animals, such as chameleons, can change their skin to match their surroundings and stay hidden. They blend in with the leaves they live in.

Plant diets

Lots of animals are **herbivores** which means they only eat plants. Some animals, such as orangutans, mostly eat fruit. Other animals, such as sloths, mostly eat leaves.

Pond protectors

Pond plants provide shelter for fish hiding from predators, such as birds. The plants also filter the water to make it cleaner for the fish to live in.

Grasses and meadows

Many animals, such as lizards and snakes, live among the long grasses of meadows. This is a perfect habitat for them as the grass provides a place to hide from bigger animals.

Insect food

Insects, such as bees and butterflies, collect nectar made by flowers. This sugary liquid gives them energy, and is what bees use to make honey. Yum!

Did You Know?

Plants are pretty amazing! Every living creature needs plants to survive; the world wouldn't be the way it is today if we didn't have them. Did you know these amazing facts about plants?

Saffron is the most expensive spice in the world. Sometimes, it can cost more than gold!

It can take **10** minutes for a falling raindrop to make its way through the rainforest's thick canopy and reach the ground!

70,000
plant species have been used for medicine!

Bluebell plant

The sap from bluebell plants was once used as glue to hold books together.

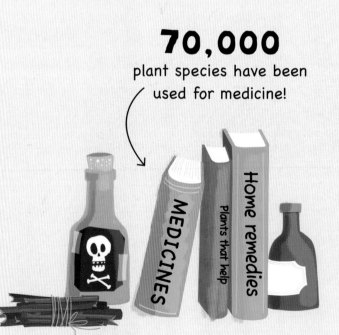

MEDICINES

Plants that help

Home remedies

One tree, on average, can make up to **300,000** pencils!

Most pencils are made from cedar trees.

Apples, pears and cherries are all part of the rose family.

A sunflower has loads of tiny flowers called florets which ripen to become the seeds. You can eat these seeds!

90% of food that humans eat comes from **30** plants!

Match Up the Pairs

Can you match up the fact boxes (below) with the correct plant (right)?
Flip back through the book if you need a hint!

1.

I'm a fluffy, white flower which can be turned into thread and used to make clothes.

2.

I'm a plant eaten by pandas. Humans use me to build houses, furniture, and even make toothbrushes!

3.

I'm a pretty flower which can be turned into a cancer-fighting medicine.

4.

I'm a flowering plant. I may be pretty, but I'm very poisonous, so don't touch me!

5.

I'm a spicy fruit which is used in cooking to add "heat" to food.

6.

My green leaves are used as a herb in cooking all over the world.

Foxgloves

Chilli pepper

Bamboo

Basil plant

Rose periwinkle

Cotton

Have you matched them all?

Answers can be found on page 24.

Glossary

Bark – the tough outer layer of a woody plant stem or root, such as a tree trunk.

Bulbs – rounded parts of some plants that grow in the soil. They store food and shoots grow out of them.

Camouflage – to look like something else in order to stay hidden.

Carbon dioxide – an invisible gas in the air that plants take in to make food and oxygen.

Diet – food that you eat regularly.

Droughts – a long period of dryness, usually caused by lack of rainfall.

Evergreen - a type of plant whose leaves stay green all year round. These plants also do not lose their leaves in winter.

Flooding – when large amounts of water overflows into areas of land where it shouldn't be.

Global warming – the rising temperature of the planet, which causes climate change.

Habitats – the natural homes of plants and animals.

Herbivore – an animal that only eats plants.

Nutrients – substances or ingredients that plants and animals need to live and grow.

Oxygen – an invisible gas in the air that plants produce, and people and animals need to breathe.

Pollute – (verb) to make dirty or harmful with waste, chemicals, or other substances.

Sap – a watery substance that comes out of a plant or tree.

Trunk – the large woody stem of a tree, where the branches grow from.

Answers to Match Up the Pairs

Answers: 1. Cotton, 2. Bamboo, 3. Rose periwinkle, 4. Foxgloves, 5. Chilli pepper, 6. Basil plant.